Teaching Little Fingers to Play
More American Tunes

Piano Solos with Optional Teacher Accompaniments

Arranged by Eric Baumgartner

CONTENTS

ISBN 978-1-4584-9431-3

WILLIS MUSIC

EXCLUSIVELY DISTRIBUTED BY

HAL•LEONARD®

7777 W. BLUEMOUND RD. P.O. BOX 13819 MILWAUKEE, WI 53213

Visit Hal Leonard Online at
www.halleonard.com

Camptown Races
Optional Teacher Accompaniment

Stephen Foster
arr. Eric Baumgartner

Camptown Races

Stephen Foster
arr. Eric Baumgartner

Play both hands one octave higher when performing as a duet

The Arkansas Traveler
Optional Teacher Accompaniment

Sanford Faulkner
arr. Eric Baumgartner

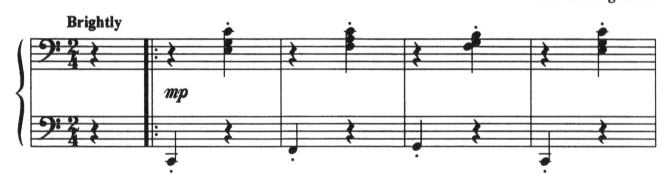

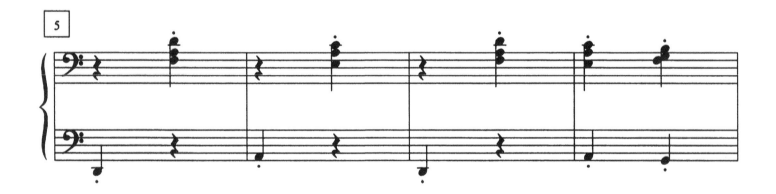

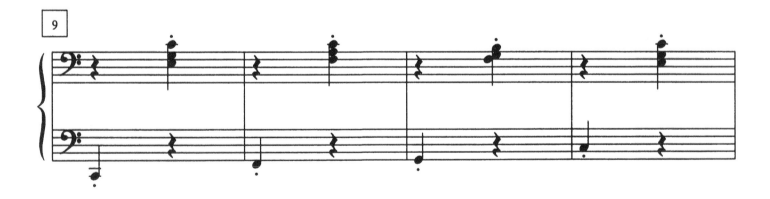

The Arkansas Traveler

Sanford Faulkner
arr. Eric Baumgartner

Play both hands one octave higher when performing as a duet

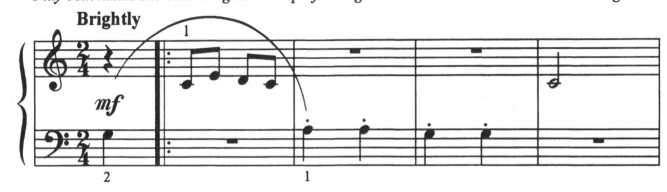

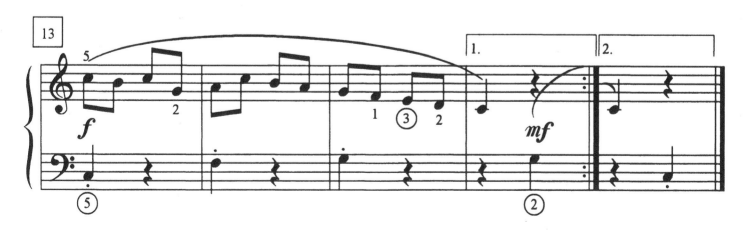

Clementine
Optional Teacher Accompaniment

Traditional
arr. Eric Baumgartner

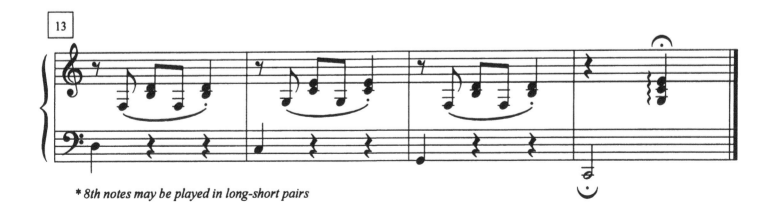

* 8th notes may be played in long-short pairs

Clementine

Traditional
arr. Eric Baumgartner

Play both hands one octave higher when performing as a duet

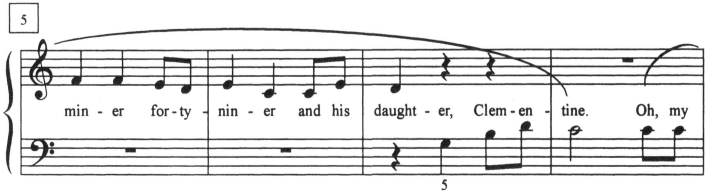

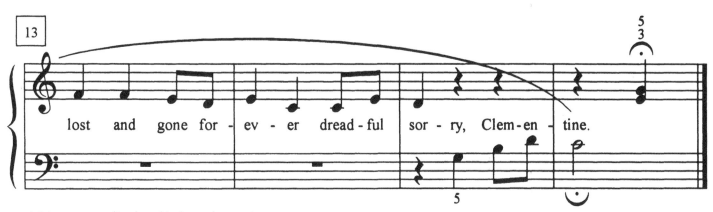

* 8th notes may be played in long-short pairs

Oh, Susanna!
Optional Teacher Accompaniment

Stephen Foster
arr. Eric Baumgartner

Oh, Susanna!

Stephen Foster
arr. Eric Baumgartner

Play both hands one octave higher when performing as a duet

The Red River Valley

Optional Teacher Accompaniment

Traditional
arr. Eric Baumgartner

The Red River Valley

Traditional
arr. Eric Baumgartner

Play both hands one octave higher when performing as a duet

Stars and Stripes Forever
Optional Teacher Accompaniment

John Philip Sousa
arr. Eric Baumgartner

Stars and Stripes Forever

John Philip Sousa
arr. Eric Baumgartner

Play both hands one octave higher when performing as a duet

Lively march tempo

Give My Regards to Broadway

Optional Teacher Accompaniment

George M. Cohan
arr. Eric Baumgartner

Give My Regards to Broadway

George M. Cohan
arr. Eric Baumgartner

Play both hands one octave higher when performing as a duet

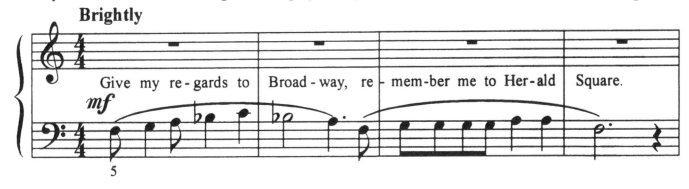

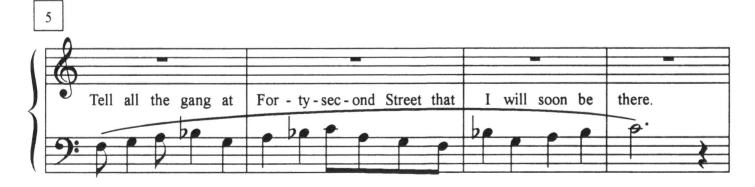

Turkey in the Straw
Optional Teacher Accompaniment

Traditional
arr. Eric Baumgartner

Turkey in the Straw

Traditional
arr. Eric Baumgartner

Play both hands one octave higher when performing as a duet

The Entertainer
Optional Teacher Accompaniment

Scott Joplin
arr. Eric Baumgartner

The Entertainer

Scott Joplin
arr. Eric Baumgartner

Play both hands one octave higher when performing as a duet

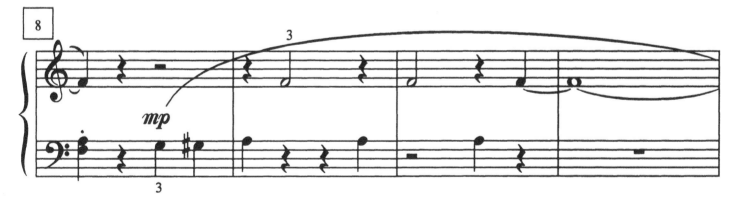

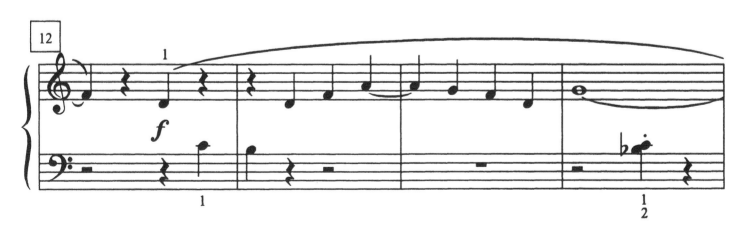

20

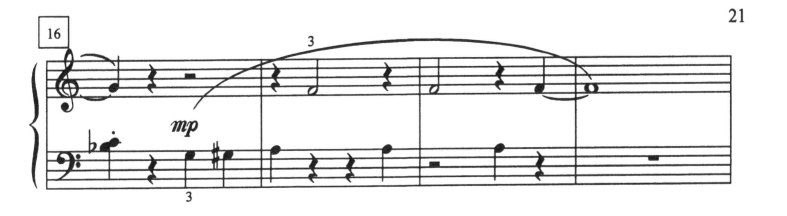

You're a Grand Old Flag

Optional Teacher Accompaniment

George M. Cohan
arr. Eric Baumgartner

You're a Grand Old Flag

George M. Cohan
arr. Eric Baumgartner

Play both hands one octave higher when performing as a duet

TEACHING LITTLE FINGERS TO PLAY MORE

TEACHING LITTLE FINGERS TO PLAY MORE
by Leigh Kaplan
Teaching Little Fingers to Play More is a fun-filled and colorfully illustrated follow-up book to *Teaching Little Fingers to Play*. It strengthens skills learned while carefully easing the transition into John Thompson's *Modern Course, First Grade*.
00406137 Book only $6.99
00406527 Book/Audio $9.99

SUPPLEMENTARY SERIES
All books include optional teacher accompaniments.

BROADWAY SONGS
arr. Carolyn Miller
MID TO LATER ELEMENTARY LEVEL
10 great show tunes for students to enjoy, including: Edelweiss • I Whistle a Happy Tune • I Won't Grow Up • Maybe • The Music of the Night • and more.
00416928 Book only $6.99
00416929 Book/Audio $12.99

CHILDREN'S SONGS
arr. Carolyn Miller
MID-ELEMENTARY LEVEL
10 songs: The Candy Man • Do-Re-Mi • I'm Popeye the Sailor Man • It's a Small World • Linus and Lucy • The Muppet Show Theme • Sesame Street Theme • Supercalifragilisticexpialidocious • Tomorrow.
00416810 Book only $6.99
00416811 Book/Audio $12.99

CLASSICS
arr. Randall Hartsell
MID-ELEMENTARY LEVEL
7 solos: Marche Slave • Over the Waves • Polovtsian Dance (from the opera *Prince Igor*) • Pomp and Circumstance • Rondeau • Waltz (from the ballet *Sleeping Beauty*) • William Tell Overture.
00406760 Book only $5.99
00416513 Book/Audio $10.99

DISNEY TUNES
arr. Glenda Austin
MID-ELEMENTARY LEVEL
9 songs, including: Circle of Life • Colors of the Wind • A Dream Is a Wish Your Heart Makes • A Spoonful of Sugar • Under the Sea • A Whole New World • and more.
00416750 Book only $9.99
00416751 Book/Audio $12.99

EASY DUETS
arr. Carolyn Miller
MID-ELEMENTARY LEVEL
9 equal-level duets: A Bicycle Built for Two • Blow the Man Down • Chopsticks • Do Your Ears Hang Low? • I've Been Working on the Railroad • The Man on the Flying Trapeze • Short'nin' Bread • Skip to My Lou • The Yellow Rose of Texas.
00416832 Book only $6.99
00416833 Book/Audio $10.99

JAZZ AND ROCK
Eric Baumgartner
MID-ELEMENTARY LEVEL
11 solos, including: Big Bass Boogie • Crescendo Rock • Funky Fingers • Jazz Waltz in G • Rockin' Rhythm • Squirrel Race • and more!
00406765 Book only $5.99

MOVIE MUSIC
arr. Carolyn Miller
LATER ELEMENTARY LEVEL
10 magical movie arrangements: Bella's Lullaby (Twilight) • Somewhere Out There (An American Tail) • True Love's Kiss (Enchanted) • and more.
00139190 Book/Audio $10.99

Also available:

AMERICAN TUNES
arr. Eric Baumgartner
MID-ELEMENTARY LEVEL
00406755 Book only $6.99

BLUES AND BOOGIE
Carolyn Miller
MID-ELEMENTARY LEVEL
00406764 Book only $5.99

CHRISTMAS CAROLS
arr. Carolyn Miller
MID-ELEMENTARY LEVEL
00406763 Book only $6.99

CHRISTMAS CLASSICS
arr. Eric Baumgartner
MID-ELEMENTARY LEVEL
00416827 Book only $6.99
00416826 Book/Audio $12.99

CHRISTMAS FAVORITES
arr. Eric Baumgartner
MID-ELEMENTARY LEVEL
00416723 Book only $7.99
00416724 Book/Audio $12.99

FAMILIAR TUNES
arr. Glenda Austin
MID-ELEMENTARY LEVEL
00406761 Book only $6.99

HYMNS
arr. Glenda Austin
MID-ELEMENTARY LEVEL
00406762 Book only $6.99

JEWISH FAVORITES
arr. Eric Baumgartner
MID-ELEMENTARY LEVEL
00416755 Book only $5.99

RECITAL PIECES
Carolyn Miller
MID-ELEMENTARY LEVEL
00416540 Book only $5.99

SONGS FROM MANY LANDS
arr. Carolyn C. Setliff
MID-ELEMENTARY LEVEL
00416688 Book only $5.99

EXCLUSIVELY DISTRIBUTED BY

WILLIS MUSIC

HAL•LEONARD®

Complete song lists online at
www.halleonard.com

Prices, contents, and availability subject to change without notice.